Of Turbulence And Tranquility

Krithika Solai

BookLeaf Publishing

India | USA | UK

Presentation by *BookLeaf Publishing*

Web: www.bookleafpub.com

E-mail: info@bookleafpub.com

ISBN: 9789358734157

First edition 2023

DEDICATION

To all the marvelous muses of my creativity.

To all the cheerleaders that I'm lucky to have in my life.

ACKNOWLEDGEMENT

I extend profound gratitude to all who played a role in bringing this poetry book to life.

I'd like to start with a huge shoutout to my friends and family for their unwavering support and encouragement throughout this journey. Your belief in me and my writing has not only been a constant source of inspiration but has also served as motivation to keep going on the days when I felt like almost giving up.

Further, I'm incredibly indebted to the readers who have embraced my words and found resonance within them. Your presence, engagement, and support have given my poems purpose and meaning. It is an honor to have the opportunity to share my thoughts and emotions with you, and I hope that this collection touches your hearts as much as it has touched mine.

Lastly, a heartfelt thank you to the publishers, designers, and all the professionals involved in bringing this book to fruition. Your dedication and expertise have transformed these poems into a tangible reality, and I am grateful for the opportunity to share my words with a wider audience.

May these poems weave a tapestry of emotions and serve as a reminder of our shared human experiences.

Chaotic Solace

Towering walls that were meticulously built,
neither of brick, nor of steel but of brawny grit
and adamance.
Thy's nascent knocks upon them,
instinctively propelled me to further strengthen
them.

When thou annihilated it gradually,
the higher did I try to erect my fortification,
but the harder did I fall for thou,
Bound by the paradox of resisting.

Was it just Cupid's play again?
Or alas another ricochet?
I know not and wish not to know;
Because in a pedestrian yet unassailable
existence,
thou implanted chaos.
In a world full of chaos,
thou became my serene silence.

High on integrity and drunk on self-control,
defied all inner-voices and cues put forth by my
heart.

Chose to let my ego take over the wheel, to love
but permit not to be loved.
But thou came along to contend,
my flawed yet firm world of blacks and whites.

Was I being incited?
Or just another emotionally vulnerable victim?
I know not and wish not to know;
Because in a pedestrian yet unassailable
existence,
thou implanted chaos.
In a world full of chaos,
thou became my serene silence.

It may be a duck soup,
to fancy her with boar oars in the water.
But to lift me from a miscellany of mayhem,
and bring me some succor,
invariably be no cherry pie.

But was it your altruism in play?
Or just another ulterior blarney?
I know not and wish not to know;
Because in a pedestrian yet unassailable
existence,
thou implanted chaos.
In a world full of chaos,
thou became my serene silence.

My Scarlet Scion

Beneath the divine, dusk sky,
Prevails a serene and amicable atmosphere,
Perpetually blanketing the aura with familiar
bliss and jubilance,
Seems extraordinarily distinct to me, at this very
moment.

Innocent shrieks of toddlers fading into the
background,
The transcendent sight of promenading couples,
struck by Cupid's arrow,
And the unparalleled evening walk embraced by
the seasoned,
Paving way to their adorable material time.

All habitual happenings,
An indispensable sight to me each passing day,
Insinuated absolutely no contention today,
Against that very captivating rose plant.
Cultivated & nurtured, my devotion untold right
from her dawn,
Showered each day with my boundless,
unconditional love.

Be it the fully bloomed elegant ones,

The enclosed buds poised to meet the world,
Or the embryo in its developmental stage.
Each one charming in its own aspect, way
beyond verbal description.

I must be so tenaciously attached to her,
That even during her incubation period,
Her lush green leaves stand apart to me,
From all other vibrant shades housed in the same
garden.

But it's truly a beautiful feeling,
To love the ordinary leaves,
In contrast to having an eye for the vibrant
blooms,
Which I think is rather ordinary.

As darkness spreads over the arena,
Tangibility takes over me.
I move ahead to fulfill my routine of monotone,
With the apprehension the next dusky evening is
not far off,
To encounter my shrub yet again,
And witness her enchanting beauty encore!

Timeless Longing

Ages have passed by,
Since the last day I laid eyes on you.
Yet the memory of your every feature,
Remains vivid as if it were just yesterday!

Verbal conversations,
Might never have been our mode of
communication.
Yet I recognize your bubbly, immature voice,
From the depth of any ocean,
From the height of any mountain,
Anywhere, everywhere, as though I've heard it
since a fetus.

Your touch so tender and loving,
Can never be forgotten,
Like the first touch of a mother,
Is to a newborn.

Unbeknownst to you, you stole my heart,
Many years ago, without intention.
And to this day, it remains captive,
Within the embrace of your strong, yet tender,
arms.

Standing alone on this vast expanse of land,
Heart astray and feeling trounced,
I can feel your breath with the gentle breeze,
Blowing on my face and drying out my tears.
And then I look around for some support,
Only to be greeted by an encore of solitude.

Gazing blankly at the picturesque moon,
Adding beauty to the peaceful night sky,
I ponder if you'll ever release my heart;
The moon of my existence.

String of Fate

Little was I conscious that I would be hers.
That she would define such an integral part of
me.
That she would be such an indispensable portion
in my life.

Never was I a believer in destiny.
Me was hostage to the illusion painted by an
idealist,
That each one is responsible for theirs.

But amidst present circumstances,
As fate would have it, all pre-determined,
I am certainly cognizant of my serendipity.

May it be a god-sent benefaction, may it be a
nemesis,
Whichever it may be,
Remains a deranged controversy for my opinion
upon it.

But all I can discern contemporarily is that,
She is mine today,
And she will be mine tomorrow.

Through all conviviality, through all
catastrophes,
She shall have a tenacious grip over me,
And I shall have a tenacious grip over her.

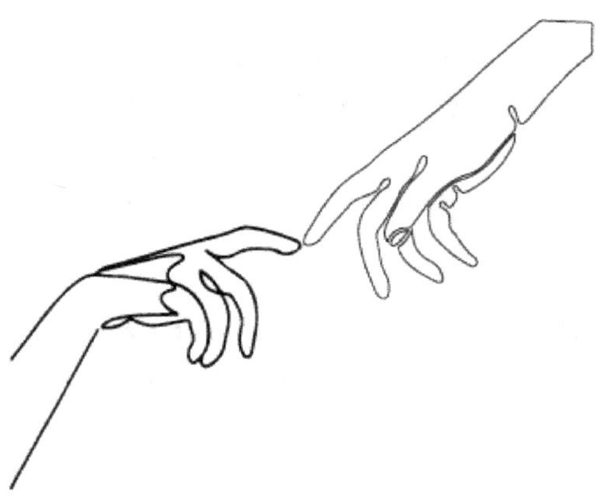

The Moon to My Night Sky

Bright, blue, clarion sky.
Waves reverberating on crashing the shores,
Tiny tots forging sandcastles,
Their zealous babble echoing incessantly.

Thou'll envisage a scenic beauty,
A picturesque backdrop for a quotidian.
Howbeit solitude enwraps me impermeably,
Further distancing any emotion,
That resembles positivity even if slightly.

Indeed, the skies seem to be clarion,
But my ability to contemplate, impaired.
Indeed, the waves confront the shore
periodically,
But my sight of my swain remains deprived.

Solitude enwraps me impermeably,
Like the tenacious tentacles of an octopus,
Swathing me hidebound,
Leaving me gasping for breath.

Solitude enwraps me impermeably,
Like a fragile vase of glass,

That was subtly tipped off from the edge of a
cliff,
Now shattered into innumerable pieces.

Solitude enwraps me impermeably,
That sights of bliss and ecstasy,
Such as the summer sky or merry guileless
children,
Fail to placate my sobbing soul, brimming with
doldrums.

Lush green mountains & meadows,
Cows splashed with perfectly asymmetrical
strokes of black and white,
Grazing tritely over the lawns with bells
fastened over their necks,
Tinkering in rhythm with nature's tune.

All an idyllic abode that feels akin to heaven,
And makes you lose consciousness of chagrin.
Yet my memory etches with his ubiquity,
Reckoning the hackneyed notion that
"Happiness is doubled when shared,"
Appears to be an absolute fallacy,
And that happiness is truly felt,
Only when shared with him!

As the dusk takes over,
As banal days come to a wrap,

The juvenile reconcile into their guardians'
arms,
Which instills in them a sense of security.
A sense that has been perpetually snatched away
from me.
A sense that I never received from my
well-spring,
But one that I discerned with my old flame.

As I look up to the starry night sky,
Reality dawns upon me.
An archer's arrow pierces straight through my
heart,
Reminding me of the undeniable verity,
That his stint in my life had hit its expiry.

Neither was he a connoisseur in love,
Nor was he in harmony with my cognition.
But little did I anticipate,
That his absence in my life,
Would create an imperishable void within me.

"Let bygones be bygones,"
Certainly, holds no verisimilitude to me.
As stars may come and stars may go,
But the moon to the night sky is just one,
An immutable one, indeed.

A Remnant of You

I collect parts of the people I know,
Parts that I cherish within me,
I drop parts of the people I know,
Parts that no longer serve me.
Regardless, a part of you shall always reside in
me.

Did you believe I would simply erase you from
my memory?
Did you anticipate that I would forsake our
memory?
Did you assume I would simply let go of our
connection?
Did you suppose it was a dime a dozen, our
connection?
Regardless, a part of you shall always reside in
me.

Sometimes, just sometimes,
When I ponder upon my sense of completeness,
I wonder if you still hold a small piece of me,
And likewise have no choice but to hold on to it
for eternity.
Regardless, a part of you shall always reside in
me.

The Gift of Belief

I cherish our innocuous times spent together,
The way you understood me like no other.
Though you've departed this earthly plane,
Your presence lingers, an eternal refrain.
Your boundless love, I yearn sometimes,
But I know our bond is not confined to this
realm.

You said I can do anything I want,
You said I can be anything I want,
You said that all I need is to embrace my
dreams,
You said that all I need is to believe in myself,
You said that with self-belief as my guiding
light,
I can silence the doubters with all my might.

Amidst the constant voices that try to drag me
down,
At times they're even my own,
Out of the blue like an angel's heavenly plea,
Your divine whisper reaches out to me,
Gently urging me to dismiss doubt's sway,
Reminding me that I'm greater than
despondency's way.

You instilled in me that kind of unwavering
belief,
The one that's most invaluable in life,
And one that no education could ever bestow.
It empowers me to conquer life's obstacles
everyday,
A superpower I still carry, a guiding embrace.
Oh Grandpa, dear Grandpa,
You made me a believer and I thank thee for
that!

Coriander Chronicles

Equally do I adore all my spices,
Yet coriander holds a special place in my heart.
In my kitchen, it permeates with aromatic
delight.
In my culinary creations, it lends its fortitude.

From seeds to powder, its transformation
unfolds,
Releasing a fragrance that truly beholds.
With citrus undertones and a subtle earthy hue,
Coriander spice, truly a magical flavor on cue.

In curries and stews, it finds its way,
Infusing dishes with its ethereal sway.
A pinch of coriander, a sprinkle of grace,
Bringing harmony to every culinary phrase.

The stalk, the stem, the leaves,
All packed with an assortment of flavors.
Often overlooked, its worth unclaimed,
In its absence, we're reminded of its value
untamed.

From curries to salsas, it finds its place,
Enhancing flavors with its unique embrace.

Cilantro to some, Coriander to others,
A sprinkle of freshness, a burst of green colors.

But not all can embrace its charm,
As for some, it evokes a sense of alarm.
A polarizing herb, both loved and despised,
The hatred behind this herb, gets me truly
surprised.

In the world of spices and herbs, where magic
prevails,
I put my trust in alchemy's mystical trails.
If I were to be reborn as an herb anew,
Coriander, I'd choose, for its essence so true.

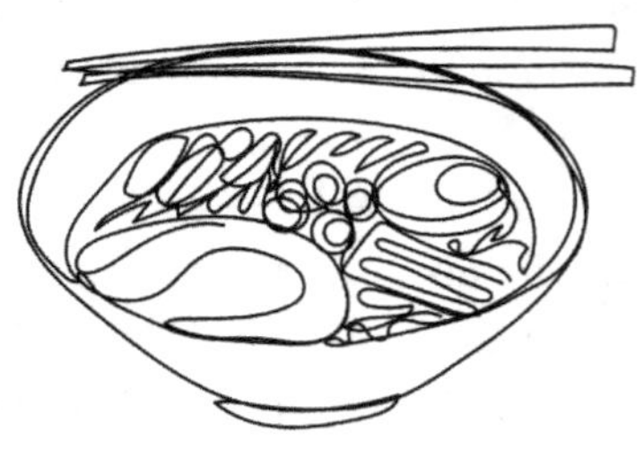

Entangled

I love you,
Or so he said.
Even though you're difficult to love,
Also, he implied.

What keeps me entangled,
I know not.
Is it unyielding love?
Or catastrophic fear?

Do what makes you happy,
Or so he said.
Do what's expected of you from me,
Also, he implied.

What keeps me entangled,
I know not.
Do I glimpse hope in others easily?
Or do they perceive that I can be conned easily?

You can stay with me,
Or so he said.
But I can't stay with you,
Also, he implied.

What keeps me entangled,
I know not.
Am I too scared to leave?
Or too scared to live?

I'll always be there for you,
Or so he said.
Not when someone else needs me too,
Also, he implied.

What keeps me entangled,
I know not.

The Dementor's Kiss

The Dementor's kiss advances unchecked,
My Patronus charm falters in its defense.
The Dementor consumes me whole,
Engulfing me in its relentless grasp.

Where is thy savior, dear Phoenix?
Oh dear, dear Phoenix, where art thou?
Rise back again from thou's ashes,
'Cause that's what you're best at doing!

Rise, my beloved,
You possess the strength within!
And I'll unconditionally cheer you on,
"Always!"

Rise, my beloved,
For resilience is your unparalleled strength!
And I'll take an
unwavering
stand by your
side,
"Always!"

Echoes of Yellow

I see summer's bright yellow sky,
And a happy twinkle meets my eye.
Like a sunflower blooming to the sun,
Towards all the light & warmth I run.

On a cold, wintery night as the Northeast's,
The sight of a yellow taxi on the streets,
Brings joy like a pleasant stranger,
Even if fleeting in nature.

I pictured yellow in my head,
And with intense joy my heart bled,
Once in a blue moon do I see some yellow,
And it leaves me feeling mellow.

Alas, even when nature is devoid of yellow,
I think of sunflowers and think of Van Gogh.
What on earth could have inspired his "yellow
period,"
when the options that lay before him were
myriad.

To some, an ugly color,
That makes them want to holler.

To some an absolute belle,
That bids all negativity farewell.
To some it's just a color,
That is part of a world filled with blur.

To me it's a pure emotion,
More expansive than any ocean.
To me it's a pure emotion,
That invokes in me a real devotion.

Riverside Reveries

As the sun descends slowly into those tranquil
waves in the distance,
Into the river, oh river, my solace in this
concrete jungle,
I immerse myself in the soft hues of pink,
orange, yellow and blues,
And Nothing Else matters.

As the subtle waves rise and fall,
The setting sun glimmers on its surface,
Everyone and Everything, seem to slow down
all at once,
And Nothing Else matters.

By the river I've wept,
Embracing a river of emotions,
Tears of joy, grief, anger, and pain.
For that which cannot be said, shall be wept.

Oh, how I feel a sense of belonging,
Yet, simultaneously, a profound sense of
solitude.
In tune with my inner being, connected and
whole,
Yet enduring the weight of suffering alone.

The Magic Within Us

As my senses soar, euphoria here I come,
A journey embarked with altered view,
Mind's tapestry woven with vibrant hues,
Reality takes on a different sky.

In the blink of an eye, to Hogwarts' hallways
I'm transported,
Clad in school robes, feeling the magic in the air,
A profound sense of belonging fills my heart
and soul,
Empowered and connected, new dreams unfold.

My inner witch unleashed out in the open at last,
I soar free,
Seeking new adventures, living wild and free,
Feeling a perfect fit than ever,
Feeling emboldened and empowered than ever.

With the swish of my wand, I summon all I
want,
Friend by my side & foes kept at sight,
A feeling of home completely takes over my
soul,
A feeling that I've almost never felt in reality.

Mind you, it ain't completely rainbows and
unicorns,
I see my all bullies, I see all my demons,
But simply in alternative avatars.
Yet somehow, I feel invincible, maybe cause I'm
now a witch?

As reality blurs, I discern the truth,
That I've always been the witch of my own
story.
Only I hold the spells to heal my own strife,
Only I possess the powers to protect my own
life.

After all a wise man once said,
Magic happens to those who believe in it.
Magic dwells within us, a secret untold,
To believe or not to believe, our choice takes
hold.

Returning to reality, transformed by the quest,
An altered soul I am, my heart renewed.
I believe more in the magic around me,
And I trust more in the witch in me.

Beyond the Couples Paradigm

With eyes full of pity, the waiter gazes my way,
As I request a table for one, embracing solitude's sway.
The insurance agent casts a sympathetic glance,
As I calmly inquire about a plan for one, taking my chance.

Looks of compassion from strangers I receive,
As I bask in the sun alone, solace I achieve.
Elderly gazes perceive something amiss,
As I sit alone with my thoughts on a park bench, pure bliss.

The holiday season arrives, with joy in the air,
Yet for single souls, it can be a challenge to bear.
Hallmark movies insinuating a need for a pair,
Advocating that happiness requires coupling, unfair!

In a world designed for couples' delight,
Single souls are bound to feel a sense of plight.
In a world designed for couples, I take a path that's my own,
Discovering myself, with seeds of growth sown.

Puppy Love

Eyes brimming with warmth & excitement,
Always greeting me with pure affection,
Tail wagging, amicable licks, gentle nudges,
In your unconditional love, lessons abound for
me to discover.

On days when the world lets me down,
With tears streaming, I pour out my heart to you,
You rush to me, offering comfort with snuggles,
And gone is my chagrin, evaporating into the
ether.
On days when the world fills me with delight,
I laugh and talk with absolute joy to you,
Hoping to pass on some of my light,
As you consistently do for me.

You speak a language that I may never fathom,
Yet somehow you always seem to get me,
Adding colors to my life, a story to tell,
You shall always be my precious, my
irreplaceable one.

You're nothing short of a blessing from heaven,
You give me strength to face my demons better.

I may not know how many days of yours I
brighten,
But you never cease to brighten mine, every
passing day.

The Intrusive Silence

The forest stands serene, its hush both rough and
tender,
Within my cabin, a blanket of tranquil silence,
Yet my thoughts blare in cacophony.
Oh, how deafening can silence be,
When one's mind refuses to be still.

Perhaps, I've grown so accustomed,
To the myriad of everyday noise in the city,
That I now possess a dire need for its embrace,
Yearning for its ever-so-comforting chaos,
A temporary solace to drown the noise within
my head.

Hope is the only thing that never falters.
And so, I dream that one day,
I shall have learned to calm my mind,
And when I do escape from this mayhem,
I shan't go tone-deaf by the mayhem within me.

My North Star

I may not comprehend her the way she'd like me
to,
Yet my respect and love for her is profound.
She may not understand me the way I'd like her
to,
Yet she remains my highest healer when in a
mire,
My greatest well-wisher, never to tire.

I still fail to fathom,
How can one possibly pour their entire being,
Their blood, sweat and tears,
Into simply raising someone,
Sans expecting a thing in return.

I still fail to fathom,
How my anguish pierces her heart with much
might,
How my elation captivates her with much
delight,
How my trials loom much larger in her sight,
How my serenity brings her the purest respite.

Molding me to face this world,
My gratitude for her will know no refrain.

We may not always be together,
But I shall forever carry her in my heart,
My mom, my North Star, my home.

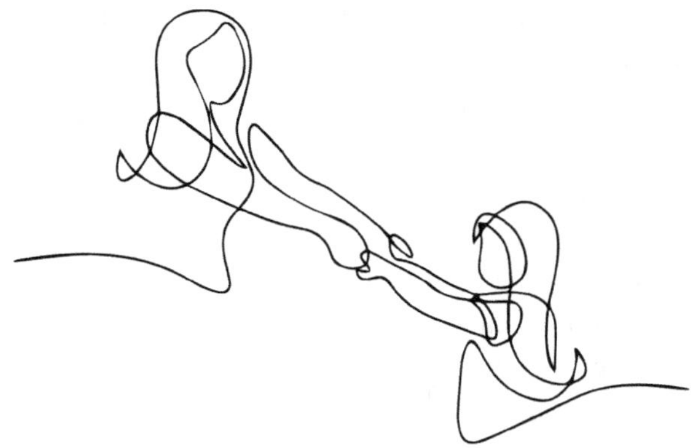

The Other Side of the Bridge

The streets and parks echo with disquieting
emptiness.
Once hailed as the greatest city in the world,
Now reduced to mere dust.
Once touted as the busiest city in the world,
Now void of a stray in sight.

In time we've crossed the fallen bridge,
The one too frail to hold all of humanity.
Now a year since being trounced,
Change arrived not as a gradual constant,
But as steep as plummeting off the Empire State.

Barren branches and empty pathways,
Still awaiting the first blossom of spring.
Despite the arrival of April,
No sign of a leaf, a bud, a sprout,
On any o' these brown barren husks.

Spring signifies to me,
What it does to the rest of humanity;
The start of something fresh,
The start of something beautiful,
The start of a New Life.

From the lifeless vicinities,
Of the prolonged winter,
Of the prolonged pandemic,
Emerges beauty, resurfaces hope,
And the world "springs" back to life.

The sight of men skipping ropes,
Of women riding bikes,
Of teenage girls gossiping over sandwiches,
Of a young boy pretending to be Superman,
Of a toddler too afraid to let go of his mama's
hand.

All banal sights that we took for granted,
Instill in me a sense of calm and normalcy.
I'm grateful for many things today than ever
before,
to have made it to the other side of the fallen
bridge,
to savor such sights alas again.

Margaritas by the Sea

Sipping margaritas by the sea,
I can't help but draw parallels,
Reflecting on the profound uncertainty of life,
Much like the unfathomable depths of the ocean.

The true depth of the ocean eludes our certainty,
Till we dive in and embark on the exploration,
Delving into the unknown with curiosity and courage,
How often do we unravel our lives beneath surface level?

Sipping margaritas by the sea,
I can't help but wonder,
Do sea creatures ever wonder,
What would it be like to be human?

As they habitually leap out and dive back in,
I often marvel at their experience within,
Can they truly appreciate the water as I do,
If they must spend their entire lives in there?

Sipping margaritas by the sea,
I can't help but feel,
The ease, the energy, the enthrall,

That the sight of the waves brings to me.

Are they deeply enamored with the shore,
Unable to resist the urge to meet repeatedly,
Yet inevitably drawn back each time,
Bound by obligations that hold them back?

Sipping margaritas by the sea,
I can't help but resonate,
The calm, the peace, the tranquil,
That the sounds of the ocean impart.

Is nature's symphony so ethereal,
That the fusion of diverse notes and melodies,
Gives birth to a perfectly imperfect composition,
One that perhaps no human can fully replicate?

Sipping margaritas by the sea,
I can't help but admire,
The breathtaking beauty of the setting sun,
That adorns the sky with vivid, enchanting hues.

Do I see the waters blushing,
As at last they embrace their swain,
After patiently waiting through the day,
For those precious moments of togetherness?

Sipping margaritas by the sea,
I can't help but thank Mother Nature,

For all the wonders she has bestowed upon us,
But a little more so for the mesmerizing waters.

Chasing Dreams

So many dreams
Burning within our souls,
Burning to come alive,
Yet no pivot, no direction.

Can we have just one dream,
Or two, three, or four?
As many as we can count in fingers,
Or can they be endless?

Some dreams we realize,
And some we don't,
Yet what keeps us moving through this realm,
Is the constant presence of a heartfelt dream.

The radiant realization of a dream,
Is like the bold, bright, and fully bloomed lilac.
At last, the reward for nurturing that new bud,
Now at the zenith of its being.

The dwindling demise of a dream,
Is like the last leaf falling off in autumn,
Letting go of what doesn't serve us,
All natural phases of our being.

As some dreams fade,
New dreams replace the void,
Since what keeps us moving through this realm,
Is the constant presence of a heartfelt dream.

Pursuit of Liberty

Miles and miles away from home I fly,
To embrace a journey of self-discovery and
growth,
Hauling a suitcase brimming with dreams and
aspirations,
Excited for my next chapter, all set to venture.

Lady Liberty stood tall, a symbol of hope,
Welcoming seekers of freedom like me, a
timeless trope.
Not only did she acquaint me with independence
in existence,
But also compelled me to dwell with
independence of thought.

Detaching from all the physical clamor that once
governed me,
Was initially challenging, but eventually
liberating,
And freedom and opportunity assumed a whole
new essence,
Right here in the land of the Free.

I hear no more physical voices judging my
choices, dictating my actions.

Sans that, the rebellious acts lose its allure,
Doubts often cloud my mind on the
righteousness of my actions,
But I must trust what comes from deep within
me.

In my quest to grow and shine in this world,
And carve out my own niche in this oyster,
With each step, I shed a little more weight of old
conditioning,
Those voices haunt me a little less each day.

I transform into a whole new person, a better
one than yesterday,
Growing beyond what doesn't serve me,
Creating space for new notions and fresh
perspectives,
Whilst still holding on to all what grounds me.